HYPERLOCAL MARKETING
HOW I MADE $517K WITH WORLD'S EARLIEST FORM OF MARKETING

DIBAKAR BALA

Copyright © Dibakar Bala
All Rights Reserved.

ISBN 978-1-63873-410-9

This book has been published with all efforts taken to make the material error-free after the consent of the author. However, the author and the publisher do not assume and hereby disclaim any liability to any party for any loss, damage, or disruption caused by errors or omissions, whether such errors or omissions result from negligence, accident, or any other cause.

While every effort has been made to avoid any mistake or omission, this publication is being sold on the condition and understanding that neither the author nor the publishers or printers would be liable in any manner to any person by reason of any mistake or omission in this publication or for any action taken or omitted to be taken or advice rendered or accepted on the basis of this work. For any defect in printing or binding the publishers will be liable only to replace the defective copy by another copy of this work then available.

Dedicated to my Mother (Sabita Bala) who had faith in me even when I didn't had faith in my own abilities.

Contents

Preface   *vii*

1. What Is Hyperlocal Marketing?   1
2. Why Hyperlocal Marketing?   3
3. Who Can Benefit From Hyperlocal Marketing?   5
4. Hyperlocal Listings   7
5. Hyperlocal Advertisements   10
6. Hyperlocal Search Optimization   13
7. Hyperlocal Content   16
8. Hyperlocal Growth Hacks   18
9. Measuring The Performance Of A Hyperlocal Campaign   20

Your Next Steps   23

Preface

A few years back, I was invited as a finalist to a National Level Tech Championship for my innovation.

The whole trip was sponsored by the Organizers including travel & hotel expenses.

It was my first time in New Delhi so I wanted to visit as many tourist attractions as possible.

My search for major tourist attractions began from Google and ended on YouTube.

Strangely enough, I found a weird & unexpected pattern in my own search history!

All my Search queries ended with the phrase 'near XYZ Hotel'.

I was looking for 'Tourist Places near XYZ Hotel', 'Vegetarian Restaurant near XYZ Hotel', 'Cab Services near XYZ Hotel', etc.

What if these businesses optimized their Google My Business profile for the term 'near XYZ Hotel'?

What if I found the ad for a restaurant located near my Hotel in my Facebook feed without even looking for it?

What if I came across a YouTube video created by the Cab Services located near my Hotel who was providing attractive discounts for a whole day tourist location trip service?

I ended up winning the Competition. Also took a trip to 13 locations in a single day!

When I came back, I started looking for local marketing strategies that can help my existing Digital Marketing Clients.

One word kept coming back as I was doing my research.

'Hyperlocal Marketing'.

Today, this word has helped my Clients generate over $517k worth of Business.

This book reveals everything I have learned from my past 5 Years of Experience as a Hyperlocal Marketer.

I

What is Hyperlocal Marketing?

Did you know?

Hyperlocal Marketing is the Oldest form of Marketing that ever existed!

Before the invention of the Internet, Television, Radio, and newspapers, Hyperlocal was the only way to promote any business.

One of the first hyperlocal marketing strategies was word-of-mouth.

Back in those days, word-of-mouth used to spread like a wildfire in a small local community.

These days a lot of hyperlocal food, groceries, and delivery startups are getting million-dollar funding.

These startups focus on few blocks of neighborhoods for the services and target people living only in these geographical regions.

They aren't being short-sighted or foolish with the scope of their business potential.

Neither they are sabotaging the growth and scalability by focusing too narrow.

They are in-fact being extremely smart by targeting people in their natural habitat: home, office, hotel, etc.

It gives them immense leverage over other local competitors who aren't ready to invest in hyperlocal marketing.

You must have been in situations where you are frantically looking for a local cyber cafe for printouts, Mobile Recharge stores, ATMs, nearby Hotels, etc.

Hyperlocal marketing is the process of targeting prospective customers in a highly specific, geographically restricted area, sometimes just a few blocks or streets, often with the intention of targeting people conducting "near me" searches on their mobile device.

Thanks to modern-day technologies like GPS, IP Address and Free Wi-Fi Signals, marketers can target potential customers in a particular location in real time through the use of internet.

II
Why Hyperlocal Marketing?

Let me start with some shocking statistics & data which were kept hidden from you.

Did you know that 78% of Local Mobile Searches end up in offline purchases?

Google has even begun providing additional results in a "Discover more places" section of the SERP, a feature that was formerly limited to Maps results on mobile.

As per Google's Official Data, 'near me' searches grew by 130% in 2014-2015, 150% in 2015-2016 & 500% in 2019-2020!

This may not sound that remarkable at first glance, but it represents a seismic shift in consumer attitudes towards real-time geolocation tracking and how location data can be used to provide more relevant, accurate results for a wide range of search queries.

Not only has interest in local search increased significantly, but more users now expect their location to affect their results automatically.

Local searches are so dominant that now 33% of all Google Search are Local that uses location-based keywords & phrases.

Customers performing Hyperlocal Searches have an extremely high purchase intent.

In layman's terms, they are 'ready to buy' from anybody who gets to them first.

In fact, despite having so many advantages, you don't need a huge budget to run hyperlocal ads.

No more spending money on national ad campaigns. This would reduce your cost per acquisition and return on ad spend.

Also, targeting a niche marketing with a small audience would get you a quick turnaround time for your Return on Investment.

One of the biggest advantages of hyperlocal marketing is personalization.

We can personalize all our marketing material to a particular audience living in a specific area which ultimately helps us build an authentic one-to-one relationship with customers in a specific area.

With the help of hyperlocal marketing, you can retarget your past customers making it easy to convert them into repeat buyers and brand ambassadors.

III

Who can benefit from Hyperlocal Marketing?

Most marketers think that only Local Brick and mortar businesses can benefit from hyperlocal marketing.

It is far from the truth.

Look at the early history of any billion dollar business in this world.

Let's take the example of Facebook. It started within the closed doors of Harvard University.

Do you think it was unintentional? Can we call it an ideal hyperlocal marketing case study?

Back in 1994, Amazon started by competing with local booksellers in Bellevue, Washington.

Today, hyperlocal delivery startups are spending millions of dollars trying to acquire local market segments.

None of these examples are 'brick and mortar'. If anything, the are competing against 'brick and mortar'.

Because brick and mortor store owners are not invested in Hyperlocal Marketing.

Which gets me back to the original topic of this chapter: Who can benefit from Hyperlocal Marketing?

Any Business who wants to dominate a certain locality can benefit from Hyperlocal Marketing Strategies.

It can be a local barbar, cleaning business, realtor, retail store, dentist, etc.

And, it can also be an Ecom Store, B2B service agencies, online course creators who wants to capture a certain locality before moving to the next one.

IV

Hyperlocal Listings

Now that you understand the importance and opportunity of Hyperlocal Marketing, you must be wondering 'where to get started?'

The lowest hanging fruit would be 'Hyperlocal Listings' a.k.a. Local Business Listings.

Google is undoubtedly the world's largest search engine.

Thereby, I am going to share with you my strategies on how to optimize your Google My Business to generate maximum Hyperlocal Online & Offline Traffic.

In the official documentation of Google My Business, we could see 3 factors responsible for the rankability of a Business Listing in the Search Results: Relevance, Distance & Prominence.

Relevance is all about Google trying to match the user's search query and search intent to the services provided by your business.

Distance is simply the distance between a searcher and your business.

Prominence is nothing but Branding. If a lot of people are searching for your business directly by your name, you're prominent.

After optimizing GMB profiles of 27 Businesses in the past few years, I have made a list of steps I need to take to optimize these profiles effectively without failing.

- Ask for detailed reviews from your Customers after they had a great experience buying something from you. If needed, incentivize them to place reviews on GMB.
- NAP citations are the biggest GMB rankability factor after Reviews. NAP stands for Name Address Phone Number associated with your Business Listing. Citations are nothing but Local Listing of your Business on other third-party websites like Yelp, Manta, Facebook, etc.
- The most important part while creating NAP Citations is consistent NAP. You must use the same Name Address and Phone Number on every local listing you would create for your business.
- Address the grievances of your unsatisfied customers and make them reconsider their negative reviews of your listing. This is also known as Online Reputation Management. Failing to do this would repel people who would come across your GMB listing despite all other optimization efforts.
- Making it easy for people to leave a review can turn out extremely effective for you. I recommend having a QR code on your Physical Business Card that directs to a linktree landing page. Place all your important links like website url, GMB, Social Media Profiles & Customer Support Email in that Page.
- Create a complete GMB profile and don't leave out anything. Complete your Description, Put up a Logo, Set your Operational Hours, List your Products & Services, Select Category & Sub-Category, etc.

- Regularly create updates for your GMB listing. Upload simple photos about your business and keep a fresh feed for anyone who visits your listing.

V

Hyperlocal Advertisements

A successful advertisement is all about doing 4 things correctly

- Triggers
- Creative - Graphics, Video, etc.
- Copywriting
- Offer

Triggers are signal that tells an Ad Platform to show your Ad to an individual based on your set criteria.

For Hyperlocal Marketing Campaigns, some of the triggers you can set are:-

- Current Location
- Search Terms and Keywords
- Search History
- Past Location
- Recently visited Places

- Local Events
- Zipcodes
- Age Group
- Annual Income
- Employment
- Competitor Brand Name
- Competitor's Store Location
- Travelling Users
- Negative Keywords

Choosing the right trigger is easier when you have your ideal customer profile in place.

Most people don't bother to create an ideal customer profile for their business.

But, it can open up unlimited possibilities for all your marketing campaigns once you have a supporting ideal customer profile document in place.

Ad Creatives are only applicable for interruption-based advertising platforms like Facebook and youtube.

People on these platforms are not looking for any services.

Thus, your creative becomes a big factor for them to either click on your ad or ignore it and continue with their life.

Coming up with a good ad creative isn't easy and takes a lot of past experience for any advertiser.

But, you can start with noticing other people's ads and create similar ones for yourself.

You may even use Local Celebrities or known faces to establish your brand in a new locality.

Ad Copy for a Hyperlocal Ad can make or break the entire Campaign.

A few of the points you must consider while writing a Hyperlocal Ad Copy:-

- Use Local Language.
- Local Slangs which aren't offensive
- Draw inferences from local events and incidents
- Tap into local culture
- Leverage local stereotypes

Writing a customized ad copy that speaks to your local audience would also make it seem a lot more personalized to your potential customers.

Needless to say that personalization can positively affect almost any marketing campaign.

Lastly, to sell any product, you need to craft an offer so lucrative that it is hard for anyone to refuse.

I was working for a local spa and we offered a free head massage coupon on our offer page.

Almost everyone booked an add-on service once they visited our spa.

You can think of similar offers which would compel anybody to get their foot on your door.

VI

Hyperlocal Search Optimization

Most people think that Search Optimization only applies to Google.

But, this can't be further from the truth.

SEO can be done to any platform which has a Search Bar in-built.

And, when you plan a Hyperlocal Marketing Campaign, you cannot only depend on Google Search Optimization to get the attention of your local customers.

Here we are going to talk about three major platforms which you can optimize for your Hyperlocal campaigns.

- Traditional Search Engines - Google Search, Bing Search, Duck Duck Go, etc.
- Social Search Engines - Facebook Search, Instagram Search, etc.
- Video Search Engines - YouTube Search, Vimeo Search, etc.

Traditional Search Engine Optimization majorly has 2 branches:-

- On-Page Optimization
- Off- Page Optimization

Few things to keep in mind while optimizing the on-page experience of a customer on your website:-

- Loading Speed of your Site
- User Experience and Usability
- Ease of finding a Page located on your site
- SSL certification and Secure Payment Gateway
- Create dedicated Landing Pages for individual Locations
- Proper Keyword Research behind the Content Strategy
- Take LSI (Latent Semantic Indexing Keywords) into consideration while writing content
- Avoiding Keyword Stuffing and Thin Content Penalties
- Inlcude Monuments, Famous Local Attractions, Landmarks, etc. in your content
- Include location terms in your URL structure as well

For Off-Page Optimization, following are the tips you need to take care of:-

- Quality Backlinks over Quantity Backlinks
- UnBranded Mentions on other website are not to be ignored
- Be a guest on Podcasts to gain a backlink from the host's website.
- Encourage people to share your blog articles on social media

Optimizing for Social Search Engines is something most people would ignore.

But, when you are dealing with a hyperlocal campaign, showing up for a location-based search on social media is quite easy.

Below are some ideas which you can implement to optimise your social media campaign for search:-

- Geo Tag your Photos and Videos while posting
- Use Hashtags that has a location in it
- Mential your location on your social profile
- Use location keywords while writing your profile about/ description

Lastly, to optimise your Videos for Hyperlocal Search on YouTube, Vimeo, etc.

- Use Location Keywords in your Video Title
- Geo-tag your video to your target location
- Mention your location while writing your video descriptions
- Use a tag dedicated to your target location
- Use your location somewhere in your Video Thumbnail design as well

VII

Hyperlocal Content

Almost all Business now understands the importance of Content Creation.

If you target a local community, all you have to do is put a local spin on your existing content strategy.

Here are few ideas to create Hyperlocal Content:

- Create Social Media Posts about Local Events like a local festival, book fair, trade shows, etc.
- Blog about the History of a locality. Take some pictures from your local museums to support your content.
- Create videos about Local issues like local elections, school holidays, exams, etc.

If you are a local brand creating content for your own hometown wouldn't be a problem. After all, you have spent your life in that same place.

But, if you are not local, hiring some local talent like singer, dancer, celebrity, etc. to create content on behalf of your brand would also be a great idea.

You also get to revalidate the content created by your internal team from these local celebrities as they already understand the local crowd's emotions.

If you have the Email addresses of your customers, you can easily personalize the content of the email based on their location.

For example, if a snow storm is coming in a particular region, you can remind them about their winter gear shopping.

VIII

Hyperlocal Growth Hacks

One of the most effective Hyperlocal Growth Hack was Burger King's WooperDetour Campaign.

Burger King drove traffic to their stores by offering app users Whopper sandwiches for a penny as long as they were within 600 feet of a McDonald's.

As per Statistica, SMS marketing has an open rate of 86% when the language doesn't sound promotional.

You can easily personalize an SMS campaign which is targeting people in a certain location by referring to the local culture and events.

For a very small budget, you can reach almost every customer in a locality and become the talk of the town with the help of Hyperlocal SMS.

Another highly ignored hyperlocal marketing strategy is partnering with local businesses.

A great way to incentivize a local business partner would be to associate a unique coupon code to their promotional material.

Whenever someone uses the code, you know that the person came from which local shop and you can pay them an affiliate commission in return.

You may even cross-promote each other on social media and via offline platforms if you don't want to pay commissions.

You can also marry your online hyperlocal marketing campaigns with Out Home Advertising.

Out of Home or OOH Advertising includes Billboards and Flyers which now mostly includes digital signages.

Make sure to have your contact information on all your digital assets including website, emails, Instagram, Facebook, google my business, yelp, etc.

Try to maintain a consistent brand experience across your online and offline marketing material by using similar fonts, brand colors, and design elements.

People love consistency and it helps them expect a consistent experience every time they do business with you.

Start a Podcast about your locality.

You can talk about the local food, local events, local culture and easily attract a lot of local listeners.

IX

Measuring the Performance of a Hyperlocal Campaign

Starting with Google My Business, you must keep a tab on your GMB Analytics.

If you don't track your GMB Analytics performance, you would never understand if your efforts are working or going in vain.

Particularly track the search traffic performance and try to improve both Direct & Discovery Search Traffic for GMB.

To measure the success of Hyperlocal Advertisements, you must obsess over the Data provided by various ad platforms.

Familiarize yourself with terms like Click-through Rate (CTR), Return on Ad Spend (ROAS), Customer Lifetime Value (CLTV), Campaign Budget Optimization (CBO), Adset Budget

Optimization (ABO), Cost per Click (CPC), Cost per Thousand Impressions (CPM), etc.

Having some knowledge about the industry standard for these data points would also help you a lot.

For example, try to achieve at least a 2% CTR with your Ad Creative.

If you are invested in Hyperlocal Search Optimization, having advanced knowledge of the Google Analytics platform would benefit you tremendously.

Google Analytics along with Google Search Console would provide you data about which keywords and platforms are driving traffic to your website.

It will also show you the backlinks which are being indexed for your website and how much time people are spending on your website.

Key data points you need to focus on are:- Bounce Rate, Site Loading Speed, Search Terms, Keyword Position, Backlink Count, Domain Authority (by Moz), Session Time, Page Visits per Session, Unique Visitors Count, etc.

On Instagram, make sure to convert your personal profile into a Business Profile.

This will open up a section called 'insights' where you can track the performance and growth of your Instagram following.

The growth of your Instgram is directly related to the quality of your Content.

Make sure to track engagement on your content and create ones that receives more enagagement.

Your Next Steps

In this book, I have given you more than sufficient knowledge to start leveraging Hyperlocal Marketing in your favour for the growth of your Business.

Your Next Step would be to actually implement this knowledge and not forget about it just like hundred other strategies you already read about in the past.

One of the best way to take action on the information gained is to have an accountability partner.

Since you have invested in this book, I want you to send me an email at hello@dibakarbala.com and held me as an accountability coach for your hyperlocal marketing efforts.

And, if you want to learn more about how I am helping business owners from countries like US, Canada & UK with Hyperlocal Marketing, head over to DibakarBala.com

You will find a Free Case Study video on DibakarBala.com where I have laid out my entire system to implement Hyperlocal Marketing without a fail.

www.ingramcontent.com/pod-product-compliance
Lightning Source LLC
Chambersburg PA
CBHW020959180526
45163CB00006B/2431